Guided Math: The First 25 Days
An Implementation Handbook

This book is part of a professional development training series for Guided Math.
Angela Bauer also provides professional development workshops for teachers in Guided
Math.

Copyright © 2012 by Bauer Educational Enterprises LLC. All Rights reserved.
1795 North State Road 9, Columbia City, IN 46725
https://guidedmath.expert or guidedmath.info

Printed in the United States of America
For information about other Bauer Educational products, visit us online at
https://guidedmath.expert or angela@guidedmath.expert

ISBN 978-0-9859560-2-8

Written by Angela Bauer
Biography Photography by Ashley Perry
Cover designed by Felicia Joyce designs

Table of Contents

Guided Math Overview

The purpose of this book is to explain the process of transitioning to and implementing Guided Math in classrooms. Guided Math is a format of running your math lessons throughout the week with several mini-lessons and small guided math groups.

Here are the lesson plans for the first 25 days to help teachers transition their students and classroom into a Guided Math routine. These lesson plans are set up into sections. Each section begins with a brief overview. The overview directions give teachers a brief description of what will be taking place. If teachers purchase this book after school has started, they may use the format for each day, but need to change the math standards used since the beginning place value skills will have already been taught.

Because this guide will help teachers of grades K-7 transition to Guided Math, you will have to focus on the math standards to your grade level. I give examples of varying grade levels to help teachers understand. Under the notes for each day, feel free to write in your grade level's math standards.

Guided Math includes several components that need to be defined so you can fully implement them. For detailed list of resources for each guided math work station or online resources, visit my website at https://guidedmath.expert

Guided Math Components

Large group instruction: This is a mini-lesson where you teach the main ide of the math concept. It should emphasize the vocabulary needed and the math process/skill. Each activity should be no longer than 10-15 minutes. Th Large group mini-lessons types are: Assess students, Introduce the concept connection/Teach the vocabulary, Model the math standard, Explain/Practice the Engaged Math Activity. Mini-lessons included the following types of activities:

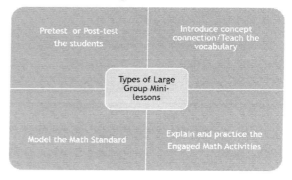

- Introduce concepts with a Smart board activity or a movie.
- Model skill on overhead or board & students model also.
- Gain background knowledge from math curriculum book.
- Visually and auditorally connect concepts when you teach.
- Make sure to show concrete models.
- Utilize questioning strategies to promote math thinking.
- Connect this concept with the previous skills or show this concept in multiple of ways.
- Everyone applies the skill in the new Engaged Math Activity for the week.
- Read a story or learn songs about math concepts.
- Talk at Calendar Time.
- Keep connecting concepts in multiple modalities. (Howard Gardner's Multiple Intelligences and Eric Jensen's Brain-Based Learning)

Depending upon your grade level, you can teach large group mini-lesson to grades K-2 every day. For grades 3-5, large group instruction is on Monday and/or Friday for a 60 minute math block. If grades 3-5 have a 90 minute math block, then you could have a large group mini-lesson time daily along with guided groups. See the attached sample schedules at the end.

Guided Group Rotations These are the stations that the students rotate through during guided group time.

Skills Review station This station's focus should be about a previously covered skill or a preskill for your grade level. It should NOT be over the concept you just taught because the students have not mastered the new skills yet. (Students can not work on the new concept on their

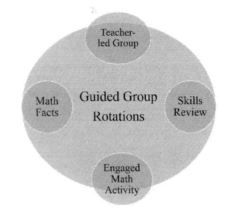

own.) For me, this station has a worksheet that each student completes individually at his desk. I provide answer sheets and red grading pens for the students to grade their own paper once completed. They grade it at the station so I can monitor this process. Then students hand it in the math tray for me to look at later. If a student does not get the paper graded, he should still hand it in. The teacher should only have a few like this to grade.

Make sure students are not taking pencils over to the place where they grade their papers. This way they are not changing answers. Have several answer keys and red pens available there. My students don't cheat because I have enforced this. (Have a group discussion about cheating. Tell them the consequence for cheating on these worksheets is a new copy to take home and complete along with a note home that has to be returned the next day. Note: Since this station reviews mastered skills, the students should be motivated to be able to do this work.)

For Kindergarten, students could practice number formation/number sense.

Students like to share their progress on these pages over the week with the teacher because they see that they are getting better. The teacher can take a grade on some of these weekly if he wants, only after the students have practiced a skill for a while. These grades would be ongoing assessment grades for each quarter.

For planning ideas, visit guidedmath.expert for online sites and resources such as: math.about.com, apples4theteacher.com, math-games-and-activities-at-home.com, and superteacherworksheets.com or just use your math student work book.

Engaged Math Activities (EMAs for short) These are activities where the students, collectively or individually, manipulate math

- These could be a math center area with manipulatives, math center games where skills are practiced, math book nook, or any hands-on activity.
- These activities are chosen because they practice specific learned skills.
- David Sousa describes this sustained practice over time as distributed practice, which is key to retention o mastery.
- "Dice Activities" Resource books by Didax are perfect for this guided group station. They sell multiple books for various grade levels. I cop one game on the front, one on the back, and laminate. That way the games last and each one has two games ready to go.
- Students play on the carpeted floor or on carpet squares if classroom has tile.

Math Facts station This station is where students practice basic math facts for their grade level at their desks or at the computer.
- ▶ K= Number Sense
- ▶ 1-2=Addition/Subtraction facts
- ▶ 3rd-5th=multiplication/division facts
- ▶ 6th-7th=multiplication/division facts
- ▶ Why? Once students learn basic facts, they can master complex, mul step math problems. If they haven't mastered the basic facts, we are asking them to multi-task with multiple skills they don't know how to do.
- ▶ Ideas of activities for this station: worksheets, manipulatives, card

games, power towers, flashcards, or computer game (xtramath.org, aaamath.com)

Teacher-led Guided Groups

These are the groups that the students are placed within that meet with the teacher at a table. I plan for that group's needs for the lessons. On most days each group works on the same grade level skill. The difference is Group 1 needs more time, more guidance, and more practice to do these problems. We may only get through a couple. Group 4

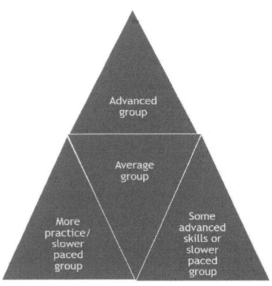

understands math so they will breeze through the grade level problems and then I show them the next skill or the next grade level's skill for that same concept.

For instance in third grade, while group practices showing basic multiplication facts with models and arrays and writing the equations, I have group 4 do the same two activities and then I have them model 2 digit number X a single digit number like 4 X 13. On the next day I do more of the same for both ends of the spectrum, same basic lessons with challenges to do with the higher groups. On day 3, I would have both groups practice basic multiplication in algebraic form. Group 1 would keep practicing that skill while Group 4 would practice it with larger numbers. With this type of planning, all the students are exposed to higher level thinking skills and concepts. Teachers should not wait until students have mastered basic computation skills to show them algebra, charts, or story problems. Whether you are teaching second grade or sixth/seventh grade, you can teach Guided Groups this way.

<u>**Setting the stage**</u> for the math environment is what we begin with. On each of these days, follow the detailed format. You will mainly be modeling

to the students the components of Guided Math, practicing the behaviors, and developing math thinking in your students. Students are building up the stamina at the beginning of the school year. By changing the method of instruction often, students are reawakened mentally and continue to store information instead of lose it.

The daily lessons will be a combination of Large Group mini-lessons and Guided Group Stations Rotations. Because we are setting up the math environment, the first two weeks we will not be using all of types of mini-lessons or station rotations. We will focus daily on teaching and enforcing math thinking and appropriate behaviors. For now the stations will be happening in sequence, not at the same time for now. In several weeks, the stations will happen simultaneously.

Week 1 of Implementing Guided Math Groups

Preparation Work for this Week:

1. **Large Group Mini-lessons:** The Large group mini-lessons types are: Assess students, Introduce the concept connection/Teach the vocabulary, Model the math standard, Explain/Practice the Engaged Math Activity. We will be using three of these types this week, not assessing students yet. The math standard for Large group mini-lessons this week is on understanding place value **for your grade level**. For second grade the math standards could be <u>NS.1 Count by ones, twos, fives, tens, and hundreds up to at least 1,000 from any given number</u> or fifth grade <u>5.NS.3: Recognize the relationship that in a multi-digit number, a digit in one place represents 10 times as much as it represents in the place to its right, and inversely, a digit in one place represents 1/10 of what it represents in the place to its left.</u> Plan several lessons on introducing the concept on the chalkboard, interactive whiteboard, or overhead machine. The lessons can be from a math book or find streaming videos or interactive whiteboard videos on place value. Interactive hundreds charts can be found on the website called apples4theteacher.com or http://www.mathatube. com. If in doubt of where to look, google "hundreds tens ones charts". Print a 100s or 1000s chart from www.math-games-and-activites-at-home.com for primary students to use.

2. **Skills Review Work Station:** In this station, students complete a skills review page that **reviews** skills. Remember, this work station is only over review skills so the students can complete them on their own. Provide resources such as number lines. Each student gets his worksheet and resources if needed and completes this at his seat. Make sure students are not taking pencils over to the place where they grade their papers. This way they are not changing answers. Have two answer keys in two places: opposite sides of the class. Leave some red pens there. My students don't

cheat because I have enforced this. They also like to share their progress o[n] these pages over the week with the teacher because they see that they are getting better. (Usually most of the groups can get their papers graded during the normal group rotation time once the full schedule is implemented. The teacher should only have to grade a few papers this way[,] a time saving tip for teachers.) The teacher can take a grade on some of these if he wants, only after the students have practiced a skill for a while.

Find at least three worksheets and 4 answer keys each on the computation skill **for your grade level.** Make sure one of these worksheets in story problem form. The computation skill for third grade could be <u>CCSS 3.NBT.2.Fluently add and subtract within 1000...</u> so find worksheets that ad[d] 2 digit numbers without regrouping or 3 digit numbers with one regrouping[.] For fourth grade <u>4.C.1: Add and subtract multi-digit whole numbers fluently using a standard algorithmic approach</u> could be the math standard.

Find one worksheet and 4 answer keys that practices place value ma[th] standard for your grade level like ones found on sites like math.about.com. Remember, the math curriculum book the school purchased for the teache[r] may have a lesson on this or a workbook page to go with it.

Eventually the teacher will begin to work with small groups during th[is] station. When students are working on the skills review worksheets, walk around to help those that need it. If the teacher has a small group of abou[t 5] students who need help, bring them to the math table so they are close to the teacher. This is the beginning of guided small groups. The teacher has two options:

1. Keep these 5 students for 5-10 minutes. While each one is working, the teacher puts a star on an occasional problem a student has correct and/or reteach as needed. Dismiss them after the time period. Then the teacher can help others. This i[s] useful if only a handful of students need help.

2. Have 5 students start at your table, not necessarily the ones th[at] need help. Each child begins working. You check the student'[s] work as each one works and reteach as necessary. Dismiss a child to finish at his seat once he can do several problems by himself correctly. Then a student who is waiting for help can s[tart]

down for help. The teacher can call another student to come over to the table to work if she wants to confirm if the student has understanding or not. This option allows more freedom for students and teacher, especially if the teacher is just beginning guided math groups.

3. Engaged Math Activities: Choose your grade level's math standard for the math fact operation at the beginning of the year, your students need to solidify. (2nd grade +, 3rd grade + or X, 4th-7th grade X) By practicing this, the students are becoming more fluent with these facts after a long summer. Prepare one EMA for this standard. If you teach upper elementary or middle school, prepare two EMAs. Great resources are Dice Activities for Math (K-3), Dice Activities for Multiplication (3-7), or Dice Activities for Mathematical Thinking (5-8) by Didax and Instant Math Learning Stations by Mary Peterson.

In the beginning these EMAs will be done with whole group or with partners as the whole group does them, but soon they will be with a partner or by themselves. For the EMA, use a variety of activities that utilize individual, partner, or small group skills. Students need to develop all of these skills for math success. Also the variety shows them that they will not always be working with another person. Sometimes the noise level will dictate a quiet EMA is necessary to use when guided math groups are in full swing later.

Remember to teach these skills for the games. Kids partner up and play in pairs. Enforce the EEKK style: (The students sit next to their partner with their *Elbow to Elbow and Knee to Knee*.) Also remind those that are too loud to use inside voices as the teacher walks around to monitor. If students finish early, have them play again. Once time is up, ring a bell and the students put their materials back on the designated cabinet. Make sure the teacher explains the procedures and expectations for putting away the materials.

Introduce some from the Engaged Math Activities such as the one listed on the website: https://guidedmath.expert I use the same Engaged Math Activity resource books in my classroom because I know their strengths in helping students learn Math State Standards or Common Core State Standards.

When you choose an EMA, make enough copies so the students can each look at one while the teacher explains the directions with them. Some Engaged Math Activity resource books like <u>Dice Activities for Math</u> by Didax have a disk so the teacher may also show the directions on the Interactive whiteboard or TV. The students need to learn that the directions are written at the top of the EMA so when they are given new ones, they know the routine. Show the students where  these activities will always be located in the room. I keep mine on one cabinet counter where the dice and game counters are always located. The purpose is so later when the students rotate through the stations, they kno where the Engaged Math Activities are at all times.

Day 1-3 Overview   For days 1-3, each day will start with a Large Group instruction component and then move to the next Work Station. Be sure to model and enforce your expected behaviors in math this week. All activitie for this week will be at the student's desk unless stated.

Day 1

Large Group Mini-lesson: Introduce the concept connection/Teach the vocabulary, Model the math standard(10-15 minutes) Math Standard for Second and Third Grade: Count with 100 or 1000; skip-count by 5s, 10s, and 100s It can be a lesson from the book, on the chalkboard, with dry erase boards, or on the Interactive whiteboard. This lesson will impart math information to the students. Emphasize the vocabulary: ones, tens, hundreds, thousands. Begin today with a hundreds chart like one from math.about.com online. Have the students skip count by 5s to 100. Then skip count by 10s to 100. This can be done during calendar time for some teachers.

Large Group Mini-lesson: Model the math standard (10-15 min.) Model the concept to the students and have the students model it with you. For second grade, the teacher could use the printed 1000s chart with the next activity. Skip count by 100s to 1000. (If possible, have a student use a pointer to visually show the numbers as students say them.) This mini-lesson can be done on the chalkboard, on an Interactive whiteboard chart, or using large index cards. If you use large index cards, write by 100s on the cards. (100, 200, 300, etc.) Pass out the cards to many students. Have them line up in order counting by 100s. Then have the whole class count by hundreds to 1000s looking at the cards. Next, use the 1000s chart or show on an Interactive whiteboard how to count by 10s from 100 to 200 and from 500 to 600. (Kids will understand the relationship between tens place and how counting by 10s stays the same even once the numeral goes into the hundreds place.)

Ask questions to the students that help them understand the math concepts. i.e. *What pattern do you see when you count by 5s? When you count by 10s? When you count by 10s from 150 to 250? When you count by 100s from 400 to 1000?*

Make sure that you enforce your expected behaviors: waiting your turn, raising your hand to speak, listening while others speak, and thinking about the math.

Engaged Math Activity: (5-15 minutes)
In the beginning these EMAs will be done with whole group or with partner
as the whole group does them, but soon they will be with a partner or by
themselves. Today's activity will have the students using dry erase boards t
write math equations for your grade level. Reinforce quiet voices should be
used since this is a large group activity. Keep it simple. For instance with
third grade, you can write 53+24= on the board and the students can write
the equation and solve it. Check to see which students can add without
regrouping. Then give them some harder two-digit addition problems that
require regrouping such as 62+18=). For fourth grade, use larger numbers t
add.

Skills review: (5-15 minutes) Students complete basic math facts workshee
by self. This skill should be a basic computation skill for your grade level.
(Grades 2-3 review +, 4-8 review X at the beginning of the year) At the
beginning of school some students may need a number line as a resource o
multiplication chart, especially students with IEPs.   The students complete
one of the worksheets prepared for Skills review time individually at their
seats. Note the students that need the resources. These students will
benefit from our EMAs. A note can be sent home also encouraging parents
to work on basic computation facts at home. Sending a list of aps that worl
on this skill will excite the students to practice more.

Behaviors to reinforce: waiting your turn, raising your hand to speak, activ
listening while others talk, and thinking about math. Talk about
consequences for using incorrect behaviors at work stations: student will
return to seat and watch others until next rotation.

Day 1 reflection: So far this seems the same as what the teacher has done
with traditional math instruction.
Day 1 Notes:

Day 2:

Large Group Mini-lesson: Vocabulary: thousands, hundreds, tens, ones, digits (10-15 minutes) *CCSS 3.NBT.2.Fluently add and subtract within 1000 based on place value...* The focus will be that students will understand that the four digits of a four-digit number represent amounts of thousands, hundreds, tens, and ones; e.g., 706 equals 7 hundreds, 0 tens, and 6 ones. Warm up by counting by 100s to 1000s. (Use the 1000s chart from yesterday for visual effect.) Lead a whole group lesson on the board with four columns: thousands, hundreds, tens, ones. Model how a number like 706 equals 7 hundreds, 0 tens, and 6 ones. Then, write a number to the side and have individual students write the numerals in the HTO chart correctly. Focus this lesson on your grade level's place value math standard.

Large Group Instruction: Explain/Practice the Engaged Math Activity (10-15 minutes) *Math Standard: Grade level basic computation*
Since this is only Day 2, make sure the teacher explains the procedures and expectations for getting/putting away the materials. Play the Engaged Math Activity that practices simple computation of single digit numbers. Explain the directions. Show them the laminated game boards. Kids partner up and play in pairs. Enforce the EEKK style: (The students sit next to their partner with their Elbow to Elbow and Knee to Knee.) Also remind those that are too loud to use inside voices as the teacher walks around to monitor for understanding of game procedures and expected behaviors. If students finish early, have them play again. Once time is up, ring a bell and the students put their materials back on the designated cabinet. Teacher enforces speed and low voices when doing this.

Skills review: (10-15 minutes)
Math Standard: Basic Computation Skill for your grade level
Students complete a skills review that **reviews** simple computation (3rd grade: Adding of two or three-digit numbers without regrouping. 4th grade: Adding of four or five-digit numbers with one or two regroupings) Remember, the Skills review is only over review skills so the students can

complete them on their own. At this beginning of the year, the skills need to be easy beginning steps to computation. Provide resources such as number lines. Supply the answer keys for students to check once done.

Day Two Reflection: The students are practicing not only the Common Core State Standards, but also the expectations of Guided Math. They have practiced behaviors for Large Group, EMA, and Skills review times. The students have seen and heard the noise level of all three times. They are practicing student and math skills in each group. At this point, the teacher noticing the students that have mastered their single digit addition facts and those that struggle. (You are witnessing the beginning of the differentiated groups that will later become the four math groups.)

So far, the teacher is switching the method of delivering instruction. Large Group instruction does not last more than 10-15 minutes. Make sure to emphasize the vocabulary for the lesson. The students should use the vocab when talking during large group or small groups.

Day 2 Notes:

Day 3:
Large Group Mini-lesson: Model the concept(10-15 minutes)
Math Standard: Place Value for your grade level

Change up the large group lesson today. Show an Interactive whiteboard activity about place value or a short video streaming movie. This visual connection will help the students learn in a different modality. Some schools with Interactive whiteboards can project the Math Curriculum student book on the board. This would even be a good visual lesson because at least the students would be able to "see" the math concept.

Engaged Math Activity: (10-15 minutes)
Have the students play the same EMA as yesterday, but with a different partner. Teachers can use the same ones over again. It is like a good book, meant to be read more than once. As part of the review plan for the year, every month the teacher can pull out the already mastered EMA skills games and have the students play them for long-term retention practice.

Skills review: (10-15 minutes)
Have the students write the equations for the addition story problems on the story problem worksheet. Having students write the equations to model addition story problems helps students to visualize and then represent concepts pictorially, a skill every students needs for math.

Day 3 Reflection: Three days of teaching and practicing place value have taken place. Also the students have practiced basic addition facts for three days. In addition the teacher and the class have learned to change activities often, practiced appropriate small group behaviors, and awakened expectations in the students. Because Guided Math is changing activities, location of students, and the level of intensity, the students remain in an engaged learning state.
Day 3 Notes:

Day 4 Large Group Mini-lesson: Model the concept (10 Minutes)

The focus is on place value for your grade level. Read and write numbers to_____ using base-ten numerals, number names, and expanded form. Begin this complex skill with an Interactive whiteboard video or an educational video if possible.

Model the concept (10 Minutes) On the chalkboard, show that numbers written in the three forms: standard, word, and expanded. Model number in all three forms. For example, 504= five hundred four=500+0+4. It is a good idea to show the standard form in a HTO chart so the teacher can verbalize the digits in the places have values. Students can write on dry erase boards or on HTO charts glued in math journals.

Thousands	Hundreds	Tens	Ones
	5	0	4

Engaged Math Activity: (10-15 minutes)

Today is all about switching up things. The students play the EMA for the week individually. Sometimes students need to practice a math skill by themselves because every day is not a partner day. Some days it is acceptable and meaningful for students to practice alone. (This is especially effective when they forget to follow the Guided Math behavior rules or after holidays.☺)

Skills review: (15-20 minutes)

CCSS 3.NBT.2.Fluently add and subtract within 1000 using strategies and algorithms based on place value... Students complete an addition worksheet Remember to try to pull 5-6 students back to your table. They may not need help. Put a star or smiley face beside an occasional problem to let them know they are being successful. If help is necessary, the teacher is ready to intervene. Guide them about 5-10 minutes and then gather some more students back at the table. Keep track of who works with the teacher so each student can participate in this rotation group between today and tomorrow.

Day 4 Notes

Day 5:

Large Group Instruction: (10-15 minutes)

Math Standard: Read and write numbers to___ using base-ten numerals, number names, and expanded form. Again teach the three forms of numbers: standard, word, and expanded. Practice on board while students each show their knowledge on dry erase boards. (Notice there are no papers to check or grade.) Give some verbally so they practice their auditory skills of understanding the word forms. Also write some on the board in one form and the students have to write the other two forms on the dry erase boards. (Encourages students to develop mathematical thinking.) An example may need to be on the board for students to refer to.

Engaged Math Activity: (10-15 minutes)

Have the students play the EMA for the week. Everyone is playing the same EMA because this way the teacher guarantees the skill that is being practiced. It can be individually or with a partner.

Skills review: (15-20 minutes)

Have the students complete a worksheet practicing computation for your grade level. (About 15-20 problems) Remember to try to pull 5 students back to the Guided Math table. They may not need help. The teacher's purpose is to give the students immediate reinforcement by putting a star or smiley face beside an occasional problem to let them know they are being successful. This nonverbal communication builds every student's math confidence.

If help is necessary, the teacher is ready to intervene. Keep them about 5-10 minutes and then gather some more students back at your table. Keep track of those who came back yesterday to ensure every student is receiving guidance!

Day 5 Notes:

Week 2 of Implementing Guided Math Groups

Overview The Focus skill for this week's Large Group mini-lessons and Guided Group lessons is: Place Value based on comparing digits to _____. Check your grade level's math standards to determine to which place value to compare digits. (hundreds, thousands, etc.)

Pretest Details: This week the foundation will be laid for using prete to drive the data. You will administer a pretest for one or two skills that you will be covering for the next week. For the beginning of the year, give a pretest over your grade level's beginning computation concept. For second and third grades, it usually is addition to the hundreds or thousands place. For fourth grade, it might be addition to ten thousands. For fifth through eighth grades, it could be addition to the millions or addition with decimals to the thousandths. Check your state's standards. After class is over and th pretest is graded, split the students into 4 groups according to their test da Group 1 is the lowest skill group and group 4 is the highest. (If you have to decide between a couple of student to put in a lower or the next group, he is how I decide. Look at their pretests. The ones that understand the more complex test questions should be in the higher group. Another deciding factor is a child who needs more time to process and work needs to be in t lower group for now.)

Skills review Reminder: No pencils allowed in this area.

Guided Math Groups will be added today! Here are tips to manage t groups and instruct the students.

1. Guided Math Groups: Begin meeting with two groups a day to get th students used to the format. Group the students according the prete results that will be given on Day 6. When students are not in guided groups with the teacher, they are completing the skills review statio work at their seat and then they will grade it. (Note: Skills review wc should be some skill or concept the students can practice on their ov

with 80% accuracy. It should not be over a new concept. The new concepts are what you work with them on in guided groups.)

2. On this day during the skills review work, pull the group 1 over to the math table to work with them on practicing the week's skill. Meet with them, have them work, put stars on the sections or problems the students work correctly as they continue to work, or reinstruct students that are working incorrectly. (about 5-6 minutes) Collect their sheet if not complete and finish it in 2 days with this group again. Have group 1 go to their seats quietly to begin playing an Engaged Math Activity individually. Make yourself available to any student who needs quick help for the next 2-3 minutes. They will weed themselves off needing the teacher as they continue to learn procedures.

3. Repeat step 2 with Guided Group 2.

4. Students who finish the skills review page can play a self EMA for the remaining time. (Choose one of the EMA's the students already know how to play.)

5. Hurrah! The students are being trained to rotate through guided math groups.

6. Remember to enforce the behavior boundaries.

Preparation Work for this Week:

1. Pretest: Find and copy one worksheet to be used as a pretest over your grade level's beginning number sense standard on comparing place values. Students should have 5-10 minutes to complete the 10-15 problem assessment. Do not give unlimited time to finish the pretest. If students need a longer time to complete the assessment, then they are not at mastery level of understanding for this concept. They will end up in a lower group because they will need more time for practice.

2. Skills review pages: Find two worksheets on an easier addition skill or computation skill. For instance, second grade's easier skill would be adding 2 digit numbers with no regrouping. Third grade's easier skill would be adding 3 digit numbers with one regroupings. Fourth grade's could be adding 4 digit numbers with two regroupings. Fifth and sixth grade could b addition with multiple regroupings or multiplication.

The worksheets should have about 15 problems and copy 4 answer keys.

Find one worksheet with about 15 problems on writing numbers in expanded and standard form and 4 answer keys based on your grade level's math standard.

3. Engaged Math Activities: For second grade, prepare an EMA on subtraction facts and one EMAs on addition to sums of 20. For third grade, prepare an EMA game on addition and one on subtraction. For fourth, fifth and sixth grade, prepare two EMA on basic multiplication facts.

4. Guided Group Work: Find and copy two different worksheets covering the standard of comparing place value. Get a binder put together with 4 different colore folders in it. I have two folder for each color. Th first color is for group 1 and will hold worksheet for them to do.

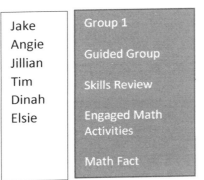

You have to display the groups, student's names, and rotations. Here are some options. The one on the left is a partial display of rotations. The student's names are on magnets they can be moved as needed. Another way is with pocket charts and pictures of stations for younger students. Middle school teachers have printed off the spreadsheet and had students keep it in their math folder. Check my Pinterest ideas on balancedguidedmath.com website for other creative ways to display the groups.

5. Math Facts Station: There is none for this week.

6. Closure Activity: This is a Large group mini-lesson at the end of th lesson. For younger students, calendar time serves this same purpose. This builds math thinking. Teachers are building their ability to apply new math knowledge in various methods for complete understanding. Teachers want to form a lasting memory for these students with these math concepts. We will be using this Guided Math Half Rotation Schedule for Day 7 and 9. You can display this or just tell students which station to go to.

	Group 1	Group 2	Group 3	Group 4
15 minutes	Large Group Mini-lesson			
18 minutes	Guided Group wit teacher	Self EMA	Skills Review	Self EMA
18 minutes	Self EMA	Guided Group teacher	Self EMA	Skills Review
10 minutes	Closure Activity			

This Half Rotation Schedule will be used on Day 8 and 10.

	Group 1	Group 2	Group 3	Group 4
15 minutes	Large Group Mini-lesson			
18 minutes	Skills Review	Self EMA	Guided Group teacher	Self EMA
18 minutes	Self EMA	Skills Review	Self EMA	Guided Group teacher
10 minutes	Closure Activity			

These Half Rotation Schedules are based on a 60 minute math block. If yours is 90 minutes, then a suggestion would be to add another large group mini-lesson of the whole group practicing the math skill (15 minutes) and add seven more minutes to each rotation.

Day 6:

Large Group Mini-lessons: Pretest: (10 minutes)

Math Standard: Place Value based on comparing digits to the_____ place using >, =, < symbols Administer a pretest on greater than, or less than. F the beginning of the year, give a pretest over the Common Core State Standard listed above. Give students about 5 to 10 minutes to complete depending upon the length of the page, about one minute per question. If teachers are implementing this lesson after the school year has begun, the find a pretest for the skill that will need to be learned. Later, grade the pretests. This data will help the teacher determine which students have similar results and needs so the teacher can pull them back to Guided Grou together.

Mini-lesson with vocabulary/ concept connection: (5-10 minutes)

Math Standard: Comparing digits to the _____ place using >, =, < symbols Use vocabulary: < less than, > greater than, = equal to. Stress the process c looking at the digits in the place value columns helps students to see which number is greater. Then give a short 5-8 minute lesson on comparing two three-digit numbers. (2nd grade)

Modeling: (10 minutes)

Write equations like 195 _____ 591 (for your grade level) on board while students each show their knowledge on dry erase boards.

Engaged Math Activity: (10-15 minutes)

Math Standard: Basic Grade Level Computation Facts Students partner up and everyone is playing the same EMA. This way the teacher guarantees t skill that is being practiced. Explain the EMA. Walk around to monitor behaviors and understanding of the game's procedures. Also, smile and breathe since the students are engaged in math, learning without direct instruction, and enjoying guided math.

Skills review: (10-15 minutes)

Math Standard: Place Value   Students complete one page that practices sums to 100s for second grade and 1,000,000 or higher for fifth or sixth grade. Use the district's math curriculum series as much as possible. This reduces the amount of time the teacher has to use to find resources.

Remember to try to pull 5-6 students back to the group table. They may not need help. The teacher can just put a star or smiley face beside an occasional problem to let them know they are being successful. If help is necessary, the teacher is ready to intervene. Keep them about 5-10 minutes and then gather some more students back at your table. Remember to bring back students who did not get pulled to small guided math groups yesterday.

Closure Activity (10 minutes)

A closure activity is added today at the end. This builds math thinking. Teachers are building their ability to apply new math knowledge in various methods for complete understanding. Teachers want to form a lasting memory for these students with these math concepts.

a. It could be a journal entry. Simply writing these numbers (grade level appropriate) on the board like 349 _____ 437. In their math journal the kids have to write the equation and solve. Then they have to write their reasoning. Reasonable answers include but are not limited to 349 is less than 437 because it has 3 hundreds compared to 4 hundreds or 349 is less because it only has 3 hundreds but 437 has 4 hundreds. These journal prompts were just made up from concepts third graders have to know for the Math Common Core State Standards.

Extra option: As the class lines up to leave the room today, have everyone count out loud by 5s from 25 to 115. Doing this gives the students time to talk out loud with a specific purpose in mind while they are practicing a necessary skill.

Day 6 Notes:

Day 7

Large Group mini-lessons: vocabulary/ concept connection: (5 minutes)
Math Standard: Place Value based on comparing digits to the____place usin
>, =, < symbols. Review the Common Core State Standard by using
vocabulary: < less than, > greater than, = equal to. Stress the process that
looking at the digits in the place value columns, students can see which
number is greater. Here are some third grade examples: 362 ___263,
500+70+2___500+20+7 (Just like in Guided Reading where we connect
concepts for students, in Guided Math we connect expanded form, standar
form, and word form to comparing numbers in different forms.)

Modeling: (5-10 minutes)
*Math Standard: Place Value based on comparing digits to the_____ place
using >, =, < symbols.* Give a teaching lesson on the Interactive whiteboard
or chalkboard on this concept. Make sure to discuss the vocabulary: >
greater than, = equal to, and < less than, hundreds, tens, and ones. When
comparing two numbers like 540 ____ 405, always explain the reasoning fo
the answer. 540 is greater than 405 because 540 has 5 hundreds and 405
has 4 hundreds. Explain this verbally and visually by underlining the hundre
place in both numbers. This technique helps more students to understand
When the teacher gives examples for the students to solve, make sure to a
several students to verbally explain similar reasoning. This shows their
understanding of the concept.

Guided Math Groups: (about 18 minutes including transition time with gro
1 and then about 18 minutes for group 2) Meet with group 1 for about 15
minutes and begin a worksheet or workbook page over comparing two
three-digit numbers like 541 ____549. Meet with the students in group 1,
have them work on the worksheet, put stars on the sections or problems t
students work correctly as they continue to work, or reinstruct students th
are working incorrectly. Collect their sheets, put them in your Guided Math
folder for that group and finish it in 2 days with this group again. Ring the
bell once time is up. Transition time is 3 minutes.

Meet with group 2 and do same thing.

Skills review: (15-20 minutes total time/ Students in groups 3 and 4 will be working on this page about 15 minutes) *Math Standard for your grade level* For third grade, give the students in group 3 and 4 a page over addition without regrouping . It could even be one that includes coloring once the facts are solved. The students grade their own and hand in. (Show the students where the skills review will always be located. Don't hand it out. Train them to go get it so they always know it is their responsibility. Also, it helps them to get up and move around.)

Engaged Math Activity: (15 minutes/ Students in groups 3 and 4 will be working on EMAs individually after each finishes the Skills review/Students in groups 1 and 2 will work on EMAs when they are not in Guided Groups with the teacher.) Choose the same EMA as yesterday. Make sure to have enough copies for at least 2 groups to play at once.

Closure Activity: (5-10 minutes)
Teacher writes 4 equations on the board._In the student's math journals or on a dry erase board, have the students answer and explain their reasoning for one or more of problems like:

1,042 __1,345   610 __ 190   538 __ 385   300+40+5__300+5
OR   1,598,321.027 _____ 1,598,100 + 221.027 (grade level appropriate equations☺)
The students can choose one of the examples to solve and write in complete sentences their reasoning. The students should work on this for about 3 minutes. If they get done early, then they can solve and explain a second problem. Then when time is up, you can even have the students share their answer with a partner (pair and share). By having the students work the whole 3 minutes, you are training them to focus for a short period of time. Even the students who usually get done early should keep working because eventually they will be challenged with math concepts at their level and will need to focus and follow these same steps. Also, this gives slower students

the time they need to complete this task and the practice to work on a task for a given amount of time.

Extra option: As the class lines up to leave the room today, have everyone count out loud by 10s from 100 to 200. For upper elementary, have everyone count by halves from 1 to 10.

Day 7 Notes:

For single classroom use only

Day 8

<u>Large Group Mini-lesson with vocabulary/ concept connection:</u> (8-10 minutes)

Math Standard: place value... comparing digits to the thousands place using >, =, < symbols. Teach another lesson on this concept. Include the concept of zero in the tens or hundreds column. The students should be "reading the symbols" correctly. > should be read as "is greater than". If they are having trouble, make signs to help them. Only keep the signs up for about one week. Also explain to **why** the children that the number 591 is actually greater than the number 476. Have them actually look at the parts of the equation so they can understand the meaning behind comparisons.

<u>Guided Math Groups:</u> (about 18 minutes including transition time with group 3 and then about 18 minutes for group 4) Meet with group 3 for 15 minutes and begin a worksheet or workbook page over comparing two three-digit numbers. Use the same worksheet that was used yesterday with groups 1 and 2. Meet with them, have them work, put stars on the sections or problems the students work correctly as they continue to work, or reinstruct students that are working incorrectly. Collect their sheet and finish it/talk about it in 2 days with this group again. Put their papers in your Guided Math Binder folder for this group. (3 min. transition)

Meet with group 4 and do same thing.

<u>Skills review:</u> (15-20 minutes)

Math Standard: Computation Give the students in group 3 and 4 a page over grade level computation. Group 1 and 2 complete a page over basic computation facts, the same one that Groups 3 and 4 completed yesterday for Skills review time. The students grade their own and hand in.

<u>Engaged Math Activity:</u> (15-20 minutes)

Math Standard: Basic Computation Facts Groups that rotate here play an EMA individually. Use the same EMA as groups 3 and 4 played yesterday.

Closure Activity: (5-10 minutes)

Put the same problems on the board as yesterday. The students can choos
different example to solve and write in complete sentences their reasoning
The students should work on this for about 3 minutes.

Day 8 Notes:

Day 9
Overview
1. Same as day 7. Meet with group 1. Remember to build Math Thinking by questioning how something works, i.e. Why is the correct answer greater than? What makes this number smaller than that number? Why did you choose that answer?
2. Meet with group 2. Do the same thing.

Large Group Mini-lesson with modeling(10 minutes)
CCSS 3.NBT.2.Fluently add and subtract within 1000 using strategies and algorithms based on place value... comparing digits to the thousands place using >, =, < symbols. Model either on the chalkboard or Interactive whiteboard. To review place value, write a couple of examples in word form and expanded form like:

Fifty-eight ____ ninety-one   600+30+2 ____ 600+2
400+70 ____ four hundred seventy   200+6 ____ 206

Guided Math Groups: (about 18 minutes including transition time with each group)
CCSS 3.NBT.2.Fluently add and subtract within 1000 based on place value... comparing digits to the thousands place using >, =, < symbols (your grade level's standard)   With group 1, finish the worksheet this group began on day seven. Remember to put stars on several problems on each student's page and reteach when needed. If the group finishes the worksheet page and still has time remaining, pass out dry erase boards and have the students compare two three-digit numbers. If this group already finished the worksheet on day 7, then have them begin on another worksheet on this skill. The teacher should check these papers. The students should have shown mastery because this skill has been practiced regularly during 8 large group mini-lessons. If the scores show 80% mastery or better for the lowest students, then put a grade on this page and record it in your record book. Check for the students' progress on the skills or concepts being practiced to plan an appropriate date for the first test. Our first test assessment will be on Day 11.

Then repeat with group 2.

Skills review:

Math Standard: Addition to _____ place value Students complete and grade one worksheet on writing numbers in expanded, word, and standard form. This will be a good preview to see how well the students know this concept from last year and the mini-lessons this year.

Engaged Math Activity:

Math Standard: Basic computation facts for your grade level Today's EMA the one on addition for grades 2-3 or multiplication for 4th grade-7th. You choose: they can play individually or with a partner.

Closure Activity: (5-10 minutes)

Play a simple game. Give each student a small HTO chart (Hundreds/tens/ones) or larger for your grade level. Verbally read a three digit number to the class. Have each student write the number in standard form. Then show them the answer on the board or overhead, or have a student come up and write the answer. This doesn't have to be a long activity. It helps develop the students' auditory skills of hearing a number and visualizing in their brain the location of the digits.

Day 9 Notes:

Day 10
Overview:
1. Same as day 8. Meet with group 3. Remember to build Math Thinking by questioning how something works, i.e. Why is the correct answer greater than? What makes this number smaller than that number? Why did you choose that answer?
2. Meet with group 4. Do the same thing.

Large Group Mini-lesson with modeling (10 minutes)
Math Standard: comparing digits to the____ place using >, =, < symbols.
Choose another lesson: either on the chalkboard or Interactive whiteboard. Today add in a couple of numbers that have digits in the thousands place (or higher for upper elementary grades) to connect to the next level and show the pattern continues no matter how large the number becomes. To review place value, write a couple of examples in word form and expanded form like: Three thousand, four hundred fifty-eight ____ seven thousand, two hundred ninety-one   1,000+600+30+2 ____ 1,000+600+2 400+70 ____ four hundred seventy   200+6 ____ 206   761 ___671
        Show some examples into the (Next) place value as enrichment and a connection.

Guided Math Groups: (about 18 minutes including transition time with each group)
With group 3, finish the worksheet from day 8 that this group began. Remember to put stars on several problems on each student's page and reteach when needed. Then repeat with group 4. If the group finishes the worksheet page and still has time remaining, pass out dry erase boards and have the students compare two three digit numbers. If the group already finished the page from day 8, have them complete the other worksheet. The teacher should check these papers. The students should have shown mastery because this skill has been practiced regularly during 9 large group mini-lessons. If the scores show 80% mastery or better for the lowest students, then put a grade on this page and record it in your record book.

Skills review:

Use the same page as yesterday. Today Groups 1 and 2 will complete this same page the other two groups complete yesterday.

Engaged Math Activity:
Use the same EMA as yesterday.

Closure Activity: (5-10 minutes Change for your grade level standards)
Play the same simple game as yesterday. Give each student a small HTO chart (Hundreds/tens/ones) or use the one from yesterday if it is not completely full. Verbally read a three digit number to the class. Have each student write the number in standard form. Then show them the answer o the board or overhead, or have a student come up and write the answer. This doesn't have to be a long activity. It helps develop the students' auditory skills of hearing a number and visualizing in their brain the locatior of the digits.

Day 10 Notes:

Week 3 of Implementing Guided Math Groups

Here is the schedule for the week. It is similar to last week. This week students are introduced to the fourth station: Math Facts.

Monday	Tuesday	Wednesday	Thursday	Friday	
Large Group Mini-lessons	Large Group Mini-lessons	Large Group Mini-lessons	Large Group Mini-lessons	Large Group Mini-lessons	
Pretests, Vocabulary and concept connection, Modeling, EMA time, Post-tests	Guided Group	Skills review	Guided Group	Skills review	Group 1
	Math Facts	Engaged Math Activity	Math Facts	Engaged Math Activity	
	Math Facts	Engaged Math Activity	Math Facts	Engaged Math Activity	Group 2
	Guided Group	Skills review	Guided Group	Skills review	
	Skills review	Guided Group	Skills review	Guided Group	Group 3
	Engaged Math Activity	Math Facts	Engaged Math Activity	Math Facts	
	Engaged Math Activity	Math Facts	Engaged Math Activity	Math Facts	Group4
	Skills review	Guided Group	Skills review	Guided Group	

Overview:

1. **Continue with the rotating format as days 7-10**. Begin taking anecdotal notes on the Guided Math Observation Sheet in the resource section. Each group will have one sheet. Write the students' names on the lines and take notes over their learning. One quick method of writing notes is to use the following notes: Fast, slow/steady, - stands for "can't do it independently or alone," + stands for "can do it independently or alone".

2. **Add something for early finishers to do.**
   Teachers can add a game that students can use once they finish with their skills review. It is a simple game. Just explain to the students the game, how it works, and return procedures. For upper elementary and middle school, teachers can have simple computation

games right next to the Skills Review Station. It should be something that is simple for one student to do and won't require a lot of time to set up. I keep several copies of one computation matching mat game next to my Skills Review station.

3. **Introduce the 4th group station: Math Facts**

This station practices automaticity of math facts. It could include a worksheet with manipulatives, flash cards with a parent helper, partner flash card practice, or any center where basic math facts are learned.

For some schools, these math facts can be on a computer if the class has access to enough computers for ¼ of the class at a time. Show students the websites or programs they may use. Show them how to log on. It is appropriate if the teacher chooses to tell the students what programs and which activities they are to complete for the day or week. Some programs are good for previewing the next concept the teacher will teach in a month. Other programs help students to master the skills they are currently practicing. Still other help to review skills the students learned a month ago to keep the skills fresh and mastery high. Some schools purchase technology programs that can be used for RTI students or challenges for higher students.

Visit my website for resources and online resources for this station as well as the other stations.

4. **Keep in mind:** This process requires a change in planning and instruction. Don't give up! Take a step back and check out the students. They are fully engaged. They are learning at their level and growing; as is the teacher. Everyone is mastering the new schedule. All students (ELL, RTI, LD, ADD, ADHD, Autistic, Average, slow worker, fast worker, Above Average) are learning and the teacher is orchestrating that.

5. **Pretest Over the Next Unit:** Pretest the students over the next unit in 3 weeks or a month. For the students that do not have the grade level skills, the teacher should send a short note explaining that these children need extra help at home practicing these skills so they are

ready for grade level concepts in a month. Attach several skills reviews. Challenge packets can also be sent home for the students who are already at grade level if the teacher wants to send a packet home for everyone. The teacher should plan for one or two times to practice during this week the preskills for the upcoming unit: Use the morning work time (if the teacher has time in the morning), Skills reviews, Guided Group time or EMAs. We will begin doing this during this week.

A suggestion is to pretest the third graders on addition with regrouping. Teachers need to see the data that tells which students know this skill and don't. The students who don't know this skill will need extra practice.

Preparation Work for this Week:
Math Standards: 2 standards for this week will be the focus.

1. Computation for your grade level (third grade usually is addition of two columns without regrouping AND with regrouping)
2. Place Value: Numbers written in standard, expanded and standard form

1.Large Group Mini-lessons Pretest: Find a pretest for your computation skill. For third grade it would be adding within 1000 based with regrouping. Find and copy one worksheet to be used as a pretest covering the standard. Make sure it includes single column regrouping (carrying over one time in each equation). The upcoming unit is addition. Because the beginning skill of adding without regrouping has been a focus for the students for two weeks during Engaged Math Activity time and Skills review time and for one week during Math Fact time, the students should have the foundational background to connect to this next skill. Use a simple worksheet page from the district's curriculum book or Scholastic has many good resource books for this. Use the website http://math.about.com for a simple worksheet like the one on the next page for second grade (Russell).   It is appropriate to cut this page in half. Use the top half (#1-12) with the number line for a later and the bottom part (#13-20) for the pretest. Remember to tell the students it is alright if they don't know how to do this page because the pretest tells the teacher what skills need to be taught. This lessens the students' stress. Remember to plan for your grade level's standards.

Give no help to students. Reassure them that this is to determine what you need to teach them; it is NOT for a grade. They need to learn the difference

Worksheet #1			Name: _____
3 Digit Addition with Regrouping			
1. 183 +854	2. 424 + 98	3. 370 +398	4. 421 +333
5. 688 +150	6. 84 +204	7. 687 +159	8. 277 +216

Excerpt from http://math.about.com
Original page contains 20 problems

between assessments. Once they do, they have learned to master some anxiety. Grade later and place students in one of four groups for tomorrow Group 1 is the lowest skill group and group 4 is the highest. If the teacher h to decide between a couple of student to put in a lower or the next group, here is the method to use. Look at their pretests. The ones that understan the more complex test questions should be in the higher group. Another deciding factor is a child who needs more time to process and work needs be in the lower group for now.

Write or display on the whiteboard the Groups and students in each group i.e. Group 1: Angela, Mike, Jennifer, Matt, Ashley, Brad, and Jacob. These lists will stay up all week. The rotation can be posted for the week to or teachers can just announce the rotations aloud. I like to post them because then if students need to refer back to the schedule, it is in writing. am training them to look at, analyze the schedule, and decide the importar information for them individually. (Good problem solving!)

2. Post-test: Find one worksheet that can be used as a post-test on comparing digits for your grade level. (comparing digits to the _____ pla using >, =, < symbols)

3. Skills reviews: Find one review worksheet and answer keys on comparing digits to the _____ place using >, =, < symbols.

Find one page and answer keys on computation for your grade level. Second Grade would review addition of 2 digit numbers without regrouping. Fourth Grade would review addition of 4 digit numbers with regrouping.

4. Engaged Math Activities:

Prepare an EMA on place value like the Place Value Dice Addition Activity Chart on page 66 of <u>Dice Activities for Math.</u> (For third grade based on <u>*CCSS 3.NBT.2.Fluently add and subtract within 1000 ...based on place value.*</u>) This EMA has each student roll two dice. One die goes in the tens place on the chart and the other goes in the ones place. The student writes the equation and then finds the sum. For example, Ashley rolls a 4 and a 2. She writes 4 in the tens column and 2 in the ones. The equation is 40+2 and the sum is 42. You can also have students create 4 columns on paper labeled thousands, hundreds, tens, and ones. The students can roll 4 dice and follow the above directions. Write the directions and example on the board for students to refer to while you are with groups.

Check out <u>Dice Activities for Multiplication</u> and <u>Dice Activities for Mathematical Thinking</u> for Fourth, Fifth, and Sixth Grade.

5. Guided Group Work: Find and copy two worksheets covering the standard: written numbers in standard, expanded, and word form.

Remember, when groups 1 and 2 are mastering 85-90% of the day's work in guided group, the class is ready for the test. Tests are usually on Mondays.

6. Math Fact Time: Find one worksheet and answer keys that practice basic computation facts for your grade level. Here we are maintaining continual practice of basic addition or multiplication facts, so students can progress soon into addition within 1000 with multiple regroupings or multiplication of double digits. I would suggest a worksheet adding three single digits, even if their sum is above 20 for 2nd and 3rd grade. For upper elementary, find an appropriate worksheet for basic multiplication.

Find one worksheet and answer keys with single digit addition and subtraction fact families, such as for 5, 8, 13. The fact families would be 5+8=13, 8+5=13, 13-5=8, 13-8=5. This will promote mathematical thinking and CCSS process skills. We are reviewing this skill so all students remember the process to create both operations. Next week, we will do the same concept with two-digit number families like 54+37=91, 91-37=N, etc. For upper elementary, find one worksheet on three-digit or four-digit addition/subtraction number families or single digit multiplication/division fact families.

Computers and online sites could be used for this station.

NOTE: For Kindergarten and First grade teachers, you may want to stay on this half rotation schedule for at least the first nine weeks. Then at your discretion you could transition to the full rotation during the second nine weeks.

Grading Note: In Guided Groups as each group finishes worksheets, the teacher can send the papers home unless the teacher is going to collect them for a grade. I look at the papers handed in from Skills Review station to check for understanding. I take one grade a week from these papers as part of ongoing assessments. Remember, the students should be showing mastery on Skills Review work because it is review.

Day 11

<u>**Large Group Mini-lessons: Pre-test**</u> (5 minutes)

Math Standard: Addition for your grade level   For third grade, <u>3.NBT.2</u> <u>Fluently add and subtract within 1000 based on ...addition</u> with regrouping. Administer the ½ page of about 8 addition problems to students. Give no help to students. Reassure them that this is to determine what you need to teach them. Grade later and place students in one of four groups for tomorrow. For upper grades, give whole worksheet of 15 problems.

<u>**Modeling:**</u> *(*10-15 minutes)

<u>3.NBT.2</u> *<u>Fluently add and subtract within 1000 based on ...addition</u>* written in standard, expanded, and word form. Teachers can show a quick review on the board. Then have students create one number written in all three forms on index cards. Collect. The teacher writes one form of a number from one card on the board at a time and has the students write the number in all three forms on dry erase boards. (Make sure if the students solve these on dry erase boards, the students then show the teacher their boards. The teacher then can visually assess the students' accuracy.) Do as many of these as the teacher has time. The teacher will continue this exercise during Large Group mini-lesson time this week. Have the students leave the dry erase boards on their desks for later use.

<u>**Engaged Math Activity:**</u> (10-15 minutes)

Math Standard: Basic Computation Facts. Show the students the Place Value Dice Addition Activity Chart on page 66 of <u>Dice Activities for Math</u> for second and third grade. This EMA will be a new one for the week. Explaining it during Large Group Instruction Day reduces the time a teacher needs during the rest of the week. If time, students can partner up and play this for a few minutes.

      For upper elementary, I have my students roll 5 or 6 dice. They arrange them in order from greatest to least. On paper, they write the standard number, then the expanded form and word form. Also for upper elementary, I would provide two new EMAs each week because older students are provided more choice because they work faster. It could be two EMAs from <u>Dice Activities for Multiplication</u>, copied on both sides of the paper. **Students should get materials and put them away for this station.

Mini-lesson: Modeling (10-15 minutes)
Math Standard: Comparing The teacher models and explains the process of solving a 6 digit addition problem with regrouping on the board for fifth grade. Next write more problems on the board while the students solve it on dry erase boards. The teacher should visually access the student's accuracy. <u>Correct, with guidance, any student that needs help or has a wrong answer.</u> As a challenge, give students a problem that includes regrouping in multiple places such as 162,589+769,243= .

Post-test: (10-15 minutes)
Math Standard: Comparing numbers Administer the post-test for comparing three digit numbers for second grade or your grade level. This post-test will provide data on the student's progress of learning comparing numbers. Record in the grade book.

Day 11 Notes:

Day 12

Large Group Mini-lesson: modeling (10-15 minutes)
Math Standard: Comparing for your grade level
The teacher will continue the exercise started yesterday during Large Group mini-lesson time. The teacher writes one of the student's number forms on the board at a time and has the students write them on dry erase boards and solve. (Make sure if the students solve these on dry erase boards, the students then show the teacher their boards. The teacher then can visually assess the students' accuracy.) Do as many of these as time allows. The teacher will do this same mini-lesson for three days.

Guided Math Groups: (about 18 minutes including transition time with each group)
Math Standard: Place Value written in standard, expanded, and word form.
Follow the schedule in the overview for this week to know which two groups to meet with today. (Group 1 and then 2) The lesson for the groups for today and tomorrow has the students complete one of the worksheets that was copied based on the skill. The students complete the paper with teacher guidance and verbal or written feedback during group time.

Math Fact Time:
Math Standard: Addition
Group 1 and 2 complete one worksheet on adding 3 digits for 2nd and 3rd grades or 6 digits for 5th and 6th grades that the teacher prepared for this station when they are not with the teacher.

Skills review:
Math Standard: Comparing for your grade level
Students in Group 3 and 4 complete this worksheet and then grade it with the answer keys. The students then hand it in. The teacher should check these papers. The students should have shown mastery because this skill has been practiced regularly for two weeks. If the scores show 80% mastery or

better for the lowest students, then put a grade on this page and record it in your record book as an in-class assignment.

Engaged Math Activity:

The students practice the Place Value Dice Addition Activity Chart on page 6 of <u>Dice Activities for Math</u> for 2nd/3rd grades. I would suggest they play individually today.

Day 12 notes

Day 13:

Large Group Mini-lesson: modeling (10-15 minutes)
Math Standard: Place Value ... in three forms

The teacher will continue the exercise started yesterday during Large Group mini-lesson time. The teacher writes one of the student's equations on the board at a time and has the students write them on dry erase boards and solve. (Make sure if the students solve these on dry erase boards, the students then show the teacher their boards. The teacher then can visually assess the student's accuracy.) Do as many of these as the teacher has time.

Guided Math Groups: (about 18 minutes including transition time with each group)
Math Standard: Place Value ... in three forms

Follow the schedule to know which two groups to meet with today. (Group 3 and then 4) The lesson for the groups for today and yesterday has the students completing one of the worksheets that were copied. The students complete the paper with teacher guidance and verbal or written feedback during group time.

Math Fact Time:
Group 3 and 4 complete this worksheet when not with the teacher, same one group 1 and 2 completed yesterday.

Skills review:
Math Standard: Place Value comparing numbers

Students in Group 1 and 2 complete this worksheet and then grade it with the answer keys. The students then hand it in. The teacher should check these papers. The students should have shown mastery because this skill has been practiced regularly for two weeks. Scores should show 80% mastery or better for the lowest students. Record in the grade book.

Engaged Math Activity:

The students practice the Place Value Dice Addition Activity Chart on page 6
of <u>Dice Activities for Math.</u> (Same EMA as yesterday)

Day 13 Notes:

Day 14

Large Group Mini-lesson: modeling (10 minutes)

Math Standard: CCSS Fluently add and subtract to_____ Show students the process of using three given number to create addition fact families, such as for 5, 8, 13. The fact families would be 5+8=13, 8+5=13, 13-5=8, 13-8=5. Upper elementary grades would use multiplication fact families. Review for about 10 minutes. Leave this example on the board for students to refer back to if necessary today because students will complete this basic fact family page during math fact time for the next two days. (Low groups complete it today in math fact work station)

Guided Math Groups: (about 18 minutes including transition time with each group) *Math Standard: Writing numbers* in 3 forms Follow the schedule to know which two groups to meet with today. (Group 1 and 2) The students will complete the other worksheet the teacher prepared for Guided Groups today.

Skills review: Students complete page on addition of 3 digit numbers without regrouping based on *CCSS 3.NBT.2.Fluently add and subtract within 1000* or grade level addition page. Then the students check it with the answer key and hand it in. Teachers look at each student's results to decide which students need some extra help through extra pages sent home or with a volunteer at school.

Math Fact Time: Group 1 and 2 complete the fact family worksheet the teacher prepared for the week when not with the teacher.

Engaged Math Activity:
The students practice the EMAs for today from Dice Activities for Math or Dice Activities for Multiplication.
Day 14 Notes:

Day 15

<u>Large Group Mini-lesson: Modeling:</u> (10 minutes)

Math Standard: Writing numbers in 3 forms   The teacher will continue the exercise started Tuesday during Large Group mini-lesson time. The teacher writes one of the student's equations on the board at a time and has the students write them on dry erase boards and solve. Today is the last day for this exercise.

<u>Guided Math Groups:</u> (about 18 minutes including transition time with each group) *Math Standard: Writing numbers in 3 forms*   Follow the schedule to know which two groups to meet with today. (Group 3 and 4) The students will complete the other worksheet the teacher prepared for Guided Groups today.

<u>Skills review:</u>

Students complete page on addition of 3 or ____ digit numbers without regrouping based on your grade level's math standard. Then the students check it with the answer key and hand it in. Teachers look at each student's results to decide which students need some extra help through extra pages sent home or with a volunteer at school.

<u>Math Fact Time:</u>

Group 3 and 4 complete the fact family page when not with the teacher.

<u>Engaged Math Activities:</u>

The students practice the same EMA as yesterday.

Day 15 Notes:

Week 4 of Implementing Guided Math Groups

Here is the weekly schedule teachers will be using, complete with group rotation schedules. Notice the two changes: Large Group mini-lessons are only on Mondays and the teacher meets with all four groups on Tuesday through Friday. Another choice is to also have Large Group mini-lessons on Friday also. (You would only meet with groups 3 days a week. This option is good for the first nine weeks of second grade or when other grade levels have reduced math time due to a school delay.)

Monday	Group Numbers	Tuesday	Wednesday	Thursday	Friday
Large Group lessons for whole class Pretests, Vocabulary and concept connection, Modeling, EMA time, Post-tests	Group 1	Guided Group Skills Review Engaged Math Activities Math Fact Time	Guided Group Skills Review Engaged Math Activities Math Fact Time	Guided Group Skills Review Engaged Math Activities Math Fact Time	Guided Group Skills Review Engaged Math Activities Math Fact Time
	Group 2	Math Fact Time Guided Group Skills Review Engaged Math Activities	Math Fact Time Guided Group Skills Review Engaged Math Activities	Math Fact Time Guided Group Skills Review Engaged Math Activities	Math Fact Time Guided Group Skills Review Engaged Math Activities
	Group 3	Skills review Engaged Math Activities Math Fact Time Guided Group	Skills review Engaged Math Activities Math Fact Time Guided Group	Skills review Engaged Math Activities Math Fact Time Guided Group	Skills review Engaged Math Activities Math Fact Time Guided Group
	Group 4	Engaged Math Activities Math Fact Time Guided Group Skills Review	Engaged Math Activities Math Fact Time Guided Group Skills Review	Engaged Math Activities Math Fact Time Guided Group Skills Review	Engaged Math Activities Math Fact Time Guided Group Skills Review

Preparation Work for this Week:

1. Pretest: *Math Standard: Add and subtract to___with regrouping*
The students stay in the same group for another week so the teacher will no[t] need a pretest for the purposes of changing groups based on a new skill.

2. Post-test: Find and copy one worksheet to be used as a post-test covering the standard: Writing numbers in 3 forms.

3. Skills reviews: Find one review worksheet and answer key on subtracting without regrouping for your grade level or with a couple of regrouping for fourth grade.

Find two worksheets and four answer keys each on <u>addition of numbers of sums to 1000</u> <u>without regrouping</u> based on *CCSS 3.NBT.2.Fluentl[y] add and subtract within 1000...* or for your grade level. One of these could b[e] adding cents like \$.43 +\$.52 = __ .

Find one <u>preview</u> page on <u>perimeter.</u> Students can practice <u>adding</u> multiple sides to find the sum. Why not preview perimeter? Find a **previous grade level** page on this with addition to find perimeter. (not a grade level page)

4. Guided Group Work: *Math Standard: Fluently add and subtract within 100 with regrouping for 2nd grade or within 1,000,000,000 for fifth grade* Find and copy one worksheet covering this standard with single column regrouping or a couple of regroupings. Find one worksheet covering fact families for two-digit like discussed last week for 3rd grade. Also know that two lessons this week will be with dry erase boards to practice regrouping. This helps reduce paper usage and grading.

The teacher must have the four different schedules copied and placed where students can see on the chalkboard or magnetic white board. These schedules will stay up all year long. The teacher must also have each student's name written on laminated construction paper with a magnet on back. The teacher will place each student's name beside the group's rotatio[n] he pretested into like the example below for Group 1. The student's names can easily be moved around between the groups when the teacher pretests and rearranges group members based on this data. The following are examples of the four schedules based on this weekly schedule. (I am only showing student names for group 1. In your classroom, you will show student names for all the groups.)

	Group 1	Group 2	Group 3	Group 4
Shawna James Ken Angela T. J. Tisha Jakob	Guided Group Skills Review Engaged Math Activities Math Fact Time	Math Fact Time Guided Group Skills Review Engaged Math Activities	Skills review Engaged Math Activities Math Fact Time Guided Group	Engaged Math Activities Math Fact Time Guided Group Skills Review

5. **Engaged Math Activities:** Prepare an EMA on subtraction facts and one EMAs on addition to sums of 20 based on standards for 2nd/3rd grades or multiplication and division for 4th-6th grades.

6. **Math Fact Time:** Find and copy two different worksheets covering the standard. Teachers can choose two EMAs based on this standard that students can play <u>individually</u> for self EMAs. IPads or computer math fact games would be good for this week.

Fourth Week Days 16-20 Overview

1. **Full Rotation Schedule:** Try running a full schedule of meeting each small guided group according to the schedule on Tuesday through Friday. Follow the Guided Math Weekly Plan. Remember to start meeting with group 1 (lowest group). This group needs the teacher to work with them first when they are at their peak learning time before they work independently.

2. **Noise Level:** If the noise level seems high this first week of full schedule, try putting out only individual Engaged Learning Activities. This will keep the noise level down while the students are learning to control their excitement of finally getting to do all four stations daily on Tuesday through Friday.

3. **Relax:** Keep taking deep breaths. The teacher is so fully engaged by this time that she may forget that this is the goal from the beginning: To set up, guide, and manage Guided Math Groups. By next week, the teacher will be more relaxed. Remember that now the planning will slow down because the teacher is using a worksheet with each group over a two day period. By now the students are used to grading their own Skills Review work, so all the teacher needs to do is check them.

Day 16 Large Group Instruction Day Overview

Guided Math Large Group Instruction Schedule
Monday Only
• 10 minute pretest
• 10-15 minute mini-lesson with vocabulary/ concept connection
• 5 minute modeling
• 15 minute Engaged Math Activity
• 10-15 minute post-test (last week's skill)
• 5 minute option (read aloud, shared math problem, or add this time to a preceding mini-lesson time)
• 60 total minutes

Day 16

Pretest: No pretest this week

Mini-lesson with vocabulary/ concept connection: 10 minutes

Math Standard: Addition with regrouping   Give a mini-lesson **show**ing the process of adding grade level appropriate numbers. Give multiple examples:

25 + 83 =	364	9
	+ 117	+75

Use vocabulary: addend, sum, putting together, equals, regrouping

Modeling: 5 minutes

Math Standard: Addition with regrouping   **Model** this concept on the overhead with base ten units or model with an interactive whiteboard movie.

Engaged Math Activity: 15 minutes

Introduce the two Engaged Math Activities for the week. Explain the directions. Partner up the students and allow them to play one or both. Walk around and monitor for student understanding of the game rules.

Post-test: 15 minutes

Math Standard: Writing number in 3 forms   Administer the post-test on the skill that the students have been practicing for three weeks. The teacher should grade this test and record it in the grade book.

Skills review: 15 minutes

Whole Group Activity: Give students addition with regrouping equations to solve on dry erase boards. Check for accuracy and intervene when necessary.

Day 16 notes:

Day 17 Overview

Guided Group Work: *Add with regrouping* Begin each group by modeling regrouping on the dry erase board for one example. Then the teacher uses one worksheet on regrouping and writes one problem at a time on the dry erase board for

Full Rotation Schedule
Guided Groups on Tue-Fri
Meet with all 4 groups
each of these days
Each guided group lasts 15 minutes
13 minutes group time/
2 minute transition time

the students to copy and solve on their own dry erase boards. Provide guidance, reteaching, and reinforcement verbally to each student as they work. Students in Group 1 may need more guidance during this first day. If the teacher determines this group needs a lot of guidance, the teacher can help walk the students through the regrouping process as the group does each equation together. Make sure to ask the students questions to help them connect the process like: "Should you regroup when you add the ones column together? Why do we need to regroup?" The worksheet will be completed in groups tomorrow.

Skills reviews: (about 15 minutes for each group with transition time)
Math Standard: Adding without regrouping
Each student will complete the review worksheet and grade it with one of four answer keys. Then they will hand in the worksheet.

Engaged Math Activities: (about 15 minutes for each group with transition time)
Students will play the EMA based on grade level computation standards.

Math Fact Time: (about 15 minutes for each group with transition time)
Using IPad would be a good motivator if you have access to enough for one station. If not, practicing flash cards individually would work for today. Another option are "Power Towers", these are Dixie cups with math facts written on the outside of the cup and the answer on the bottom. Students

say the problem and check the answer. The cups the student gets correct can be stacked to make a tower. The incorrect ones go back to the stack to practice. (See on my website)

Day 17 Notes:

Day 18

Guided Group Work: (about 15 minutes for each group with transition time
3.NBT.2.Fluently add and subtract within 1000 with regrouping. Begin each
group by modeling regrouping on the dry erase board for problem number
one of the worksheet from yesterday and then have the student's begin
completing the worksheet with pencils. Provide guidance, reteaching, and
reinforcement verbally to each student as they work. Draw stars beside a
couple of problems done correctly. Depending on the length of the
worksheet, the students may not finish it today. If not, then the teacher
should collect the worksheets to finish on the next day.

Skills reviews: (about 15 minutes for each group with transition time)
Math Standard: add and subtract Use addition of money without regrouping
or with simple regrouping for upper elementary. The students complete,
grade, and hand it in.

Engaged Math Activities: (about 15 minutes for each group with transition
time)
Students play the same addition or multiplication EMA as yesterday. Add
this rule for today: Students must play with a different partner than
yesterday.

Math Fact Time: (about 15 minutes for each group with transition time)
Have the students play an individual Engaged Math Activity today.

Day 18 Notes:

Day 19

<u>Guided Group Work:</u> (about 15 minutes for each group with transition time)
Math Standard: Add with regrouping Begin each group by modeling regrouping on the dry erase board for one of the equation from yesterday's worksheet and then have the student's begin completing the worksheet with pencils. Provide guidance, reteaching, and reinforcement verbally to each student as they work. Draw stars beside a couple of problems done correctly. If a group did not finish the worksheet yesterday, they finish it today. If a group did finish it yesterday, then provide differentiation by giving this group some addition equations with multiple regroupings on dry erase boards. If any group finishes the worksheet and has extra time, provide more examples on dry erase boards for individuals or the whole group.

<u>Skills reviews:</u>

Math Standard: Subtract without regrouping or not much regrouping for higher grade levels Students complete and grade this. When you hand it out, remember to remind them of the rule in subtracting: when the top digit is larger than the bottom digit, just subtract.

<u>Engaged Math Activities:</u>

Students play a subtraction EMA today and tomorrow. This new EMA was practiced on Monday during Large Group Instruction.

<u>Math Fact Time:</u>

Students complete and grade one worksheet covering the standard.
Day 19 Notes:

Day 20

Guided Group Work: (about 15 minutes for each group with transition time)
Math *Standard: Add with regroupings* Begin each group by modeling on a
dry erase board the skill needed for the students to complete the worksheet
covering fact families for two-digit numbers. Then the students should begin
completing it with the teacher's guidance, reteaching, and reinforcement. If
the groups finish early, use dry erase boards to have them practice double
column regrouping.

      We have been teaching many concepts of addition together: addition
with and without regrouping, adding money, adding perimeter, place value
as addition equations, single digit fact families and now double digit fact
families. Because we are teaching different forms of addition to the children
instead of only one form at a time, the students learn that math is more
connected than they originally thought. This trains the students to always try
to connect one concept in math to another, or as I call it...builds
mathematical thinking.

Skills reviews:
Math Standard: Add and subtract Students complete, grade, and hand in
the <u>preview</u> page on perimeter. Remind the students the meaning of the
vocabulary word "<u>perimeter</u>": Adding the sum of all the sides.

Engaged Learning Activities:
Students play the subtraction or division EMA like yesterday.

Math Fact Time:
The students play an individual math fact activity. (IPads, computers, power
towers)

Week 5 of Implementing Guided Math Groups

Overview

Continue to follow the full rotation schedule. The students have been trained and are following the rotations. The teacher is planning for a main focus skill for the week and building mathematical thinking during Guided Math Group time. Also the teacher is planning ongoing practice of basic math fact skills during Math Fact time and Engaged Math Activity time, reviewing skills continually during Skills Review time, and connecting it all together during Large Group Instruction time. The math time is well balanced for learning.

Preparation Work for this Week and Beyond:

1. Pretest: None for this week since the skill focus is the same as last week. This means the teacher does not need to rearrange the student's names by the Group's schedules. Just tell the students they are in the same groups as last week.

For future planning, follow the pattern of pretesting when a new concept is being introduced for the week. The next pretest will be identifying coins and adding money or rounding to the nearest 10s or 100s, which depends on the order the teacher chooses. When the teacher decides the class is ready to move to the next skill, administer the pretest.

2. Post-test: Choose a post-test on one of the skills practiced for several weeks: *Adding without regrouping for 2nd/3rd grades or adding with a couple of regroupings for 4th/5th grades.* Grade and record in the record book.

For future planning, continue to give post-tests weekly or bi-weekly on the skills that have been practiced for several weeks. This data gives valuable information about student progress and mastery.

3. Skills reviews: *Math Standard: fluently add and subtract within 1000 or…* Find two worksheets and answer keys on adding without regrouping. After checking the students' work on one of these worksheets, the teacher can record a grade from one of these papers in the record book. These pages could cover concepts like rewriting horizontal addition problem vertically and then solving or solving addition word problems.

Find one worksheet on adding money without regrouping ($3.52+$6.17=), and one worksheet practicing addition without regrouping i story problem format for 2nd and 3rd grades. For 4th/5th grades addition with several regroupings is appropriate. Use the district math curriculum books o look on sites like: math.about.com or apples4theteacher.com. Notice we ar Building Mathematical Thinking by showing the skill in different forms.

For future planning, remember to Build Mathematical Thinking. Also remember that the students must complete the Skills Reviews individually since the teacher is in Guided Math Groups, so these pages must be without regrouping until the skill of regrouping has been practiced for several weeks. Try relating *3.NBT.2* to *3.MD.3 Solve one- and two-step "how many more" and "how many less" problems using information presented in scaled bar graphs* and find Skills Reviews about bar graphs and their data. Try relating 3.NBT.2 to *3.MD.4* and *3.MD.8* and find Skills Reviews in word problem format that add lengths like adding the known already measured sides of shapes to find perimeter. I hope this example helps you see how to practice the current concept in different ways. Of course you will do this for your grade level. For Kindergarten, put activities in this station that practice their number sense, like pages tracing the number 5 in standard form, word form, and coloring in 5 items.

4. Engaged Math Activities: Prepare an EMA on subtraction facts and an EMA on addition of coins based on: *CCSS 2.OA.2. Fluently add and subtract within 20 using mental strategies. By end of Grade 2, know from memory all sums of two one-digit numbers.* Dice Activities for Subtraction and Dice Activities for Money by Didax have several good EMAs for this Common Core State Standard. Another option would be to prepare an EMA about Multiplying by 2s so you can relate it to addition concept of adding doubles. For upper elementary, prepare two EMAs according to your standards.

For future planning, continue to prepare more EMAs that practice basic skills or review skills. Vary the type between individual use and partner use. Also, Instant Math Learning Stations by Mary Peterson are good resources for EMAs for all grade levels.

5. Guided Group Work: This week find 3 worksheets with answer keys. One worksheet should continue with addition. A second worksheet should be more complex addition to use with group 4 and maybe 3 when they show mastery. A third worksheet would incorporate addition of money for your grade level. For example, _3.NBT.2 Fluently add and subtract within 1000. . .with regrouping._ Find and copy one worksheet with regrouping in one column and one worksheet with regrouping that adds three two-digit numbers. Find one worksheet with double column regrouping to use with Group 4 when they show mastery of regrouping with one column. Also find one worksheet on coin identification and adding change that can be done with the teacher's guidance if necessary. This page will help continue the preview process of practicing preskills before they are needed.

For future planning, use a variety of activities using dry erase boards, hands-on manipulatives, and worksheets that practice the main focus skill for the week. Make sure to verbally connect the main focus skill to different forms like algebra, story problem form, chart format, and picture representation consistently to build Mathematical Thinking.

6. Math Facts Time: The teacher can decide the combination of practice styles for this week. Choose from worksheets, practicing flash cards individually or with a partner, and computer games for the students to use during this time.

7. Large Group Instruction: For future planning, continue to incorporate the components to explain and model the main focus skill. Also during this time, teachers can connect skills or preview upcoming skills as they are related to the main focus skill. Remember to include videos for visual learning.

For single classroom use only

NOTE: I have filled in Days 21 and 22. You have planned for Days 23, 24, and 25 with the overview above. I will provide the format below and you can fill in your lessons.

Guided Math Large Group Instruction Schedule
Monday Only
<ul><li>10 minute pretest</li><li>10-15 minute mini-lesson with vocabulary/ concept connection</li><li>5 minute modeling</li><li>10-15 minute Engaged Math Activity</li><li>10-15 minutes post-test (last week's skill)</li><li>5-10 minute option (read aloud, shared math problem, or add this time to a preceding mini-lesson time)</li><li>60 total minutes</li></ul>

Day 21

Pretest:
There is no pretest for this week.

Mini-lesson with vocabulary/ concept connection: 5 minutes
CCSS3.NBT.2. Fluently adding and subtracting within 1000s... with regrouping. Model this skill by adding three two-digit numbers that use regrouping. This practices another standard: *2.NBT.6 Add up to four two-digit numbers using strategies based on place value, properties of operations, and/or the relationship between addition and subtraction.* For upper elementary, add three six-digit numbers according to your grade level standards.

Modeling: 10 minutes
The teacher should write three two-digit numbers using regrouping on the board. (Same type as above) Have the students practice examples on dry erase boards. The students should keep the dry erase boards for a later activity.

Post-test: 15 minutes
Administer the post-test the teacher chose over grade level *math standard: Addition without regrouping.* Grade later and record in the record book.

Mini-lesson with vocabulary/ concept connection: 10 minutes
Stream a video or show an interactive whiteboard movie on the next upcoming skill. If it is coin identification and values, then here are some ideas. Teachers could also use the student's math book so they can look at the textbook pages on this skill. Another option would be to read a library book over coins and their values. If the next topic is rounding, then show a video or look at the textbook pages on it. This preview is building background knowledge for later connections.

Mini-lesson Option: 10 minutes

3.NBT.2 _Fluently add and subtract within 1000 using strategies based on place value, properties of operations, and/or the relationship between addition and subtraction._ Using the same equations from the last week's Large Group Instruction, explain and show the fact families for these numbers on the chalkboard. This lesson's focus is to demonstrate addition/ subtraction relationships in fact family form

Give this to students   25 + 83= They write these facts:

25 + 83 = 108   83 + 25 = 108

108 – 25 = 83   108 – 83 = 25

Give students these:

$$64 \\ + 17$$

$$9 \\ +75$$

with two-digit or larger numbers. Have the students write the fact families on their dry erase boards for the other two problems. This may seem like an advanced skill. However, this mini-lesson is focused around teacher guidance. The purpose is to expose the students to higher order connection with guided practice over an extended period of time, which can lead to complete understanding and mastery.

Engaged Math Activities:

Use the EMAs for your grade level standards that you prepared for this week. For example,_CCSS 2.OA.2. Fluently add and subtract within 20 using mental strategies. By end of Grade 2, know from memory all sums of two one-digit numbers._ Explain the EMAs on subtracting. If there is time, then the students can play it today. If not, then they understand the game format to play the rest of the week.

Day 21 Notes:

Day 22

Guided Group Work: (about 15 minutes for each group with transition time)
Work on one worksheet with regrouping. Since this is the second week practicing this skill, hand out the worksheet and have the students begin to work on it immediately. The students work at their own pace, and the teacher guides, reteaches, and reinforces consistently.

Skills reviews:
Students complete and grade the worksheet on adding without regrouping. Tomorrow the students will complete the other worksheet like this one. After checking the students' work on the second of these worksheets, the teacher can record a grade from one of these papers in the record book.

Engaged Math Activities:
Students play an EMA.

Math Fact Time:
Students can practice on a worksheet or individually with flash cards.
Day 22 Notes:

Day 23
Guided Group Work:

Skills reviews:

Engaged Math Activities:

Math Fact Time:

Day 24
Guided Group Work:

Skills reviews:

Engaged Math Activities:

Math Fact Time:

Day 25

Guided Group Work:

Skills reviews:

Engaged Math Activities:

Math Fact Time:

Beyond the 25 Days

    As the teacher continues using the Guided Math Schedule for this yea he/she can continue on their own.

    To add more differentiation, Skills Review work station could have tw different worksheets at it: one for groups 1 and 2 while another is for group 3 and 4.

    After the second month of Guided Math, teachers can have several different Engaged Math Activities for the students to choose from for more differentiation.

    For more ideas and resources, visit my website: https://guidedmath.expert You can also register your email to receive monthly Guided math information.

Guided Math professional development trainings are available. Check out that section of my website for further detailed training in Guided Math.

Works Cited

Bauer, Angela. 3 August 2010<http:balancedguidedmath.com>

Dalton, J. & Smith, D. *"Applying Bloom's Taxonomy."* 3 August
    2011<http://www.teachers.ash.org.au/researchskills/dalton.htm# knowledge>

Delani, Chet, Mary Saltus, Diane Neison, Marcia Fitzgerald, and Karen Moore. Dice
    Activities for Math. Rowley: Didax, 2009.

Delani, Chet, Mary Saltus, Diane Neison, Marcia Fitzgerald, and Karen Moore. Dice
    Activities for Money. Rowley: Didax, 2009.

Delani, Chet, Mary Saltus, Diane Neison, Marcia Fitzgerald, and Karen Moore. Dice
    Activities for Subtraction. Rowley: Didax, 2009.

Fountas, Irene and Gay Pinnell. Guided Reading: Good First Teaching for All Children.
    New Hampshire: Heinemann, 1966.

"Hundreds Chart." 2 May 2012 <http://www.mathatube.com>.

Jensen, Eric. Brain-Based Learning. California: Turning Point Publishing, 1966.

Lane, Carla. *"Multiple Intelligences."* The Distance Learning Technology Resource
    Guide. 20 July 2011 <http://www.tecweb.org/styles/gardner.html>.

Marzano, Robert and John Kendall. Designing Standards-Based Districts, Schools, and
    Classrooms. Colorado: Mid-Continent Regional Educational Laboratory, 1996.

McMillan, James. Classroom Assessment: Principles and Practice for Effective Instruction.
    New York: Pearson, 2004.

McTighe, Jay, and Grant Wiggins. The Understanding by Design Handbook. Virginia:
    Association for Supervision and Curriculum Development, 1999.

Miller, Judy. "Math Worksheets." 20 July 2012 < www.apples4theteacher.com>

Myhre, Dacia. "1000 Charts." 20 July 2012 <www.math-games-and-activites-at-
    home.com>.

National Governors Association Center for Best Practices and Council of Chief State
    School Officers. *"Common Core State Standards Initiative."* National Governors
    Association Center for Best Practices and Council of Chief State School Officers,
    2010. Web. 2 May 2012 <http://www.corestandards.org/>.

Peterson, Mary. Instant Math Learning Stations. Teacher Treasures, 2010.

Russell, Deb. "Worksheets." 20 July 2012 <math.about.com>

Stover, Elizabeth. *"How to Use Math Manipulatives in the Classroom."* 5 April 2011. < http://www.ehow.com>.

Sousa, David. How The Brain Learns Mathematics. California: Corwin Press, 2008.

Guided Math Half Rotation Schedule

Monday	Tuesday	Wednesday	Thursday	Friday	
Large Group Mini-lessons	Large Group Mini-lessons	Large Group Mini-lessons	Large Group Mini-lessons	Large Group Mini-lessons	
Pretests, Vocabulary and concept connection, Modeling, EMA time, Post-tests	Guided Group	Skills review	Guided Group	Skills review	Group 1
	Math Facts	Engaged Math Activity	Math Facts	Engaged Math Activity	
	Math Facts	Engaged Math Activity	Math Facts	Engaged Math Activity	Group 2
	Guided Group	Skills review	Guided Group	Skills review	
	Skills review	Guided Group	Skills review	Guided Group	Group 3
	Engaged Math Activity	Math Facts	Engaged Math Activity	Math Facts	
	Engaged Math Activity	Math Facts	Engaged Math Activity	Math Facts	Group4
	Skills review	Guided Group	Skills review	Guided Group	

Guided Math Weekly Rotation Schedule

Monday	Group Numbers	Tuesday	Wednesday	Thursday	Friday
Large Group Mini-lessons for whole class	Group 1	Guided Group	Guided Group	Guided Group	Guided Group
		Skills Review	Skills Review	Skills Review	Skills Review
Pretests, Vocabulary and concept connection, Modeling, EMA time, Post-tests		Engaged Math Activities	Engaged Math Activities	Engaged Math Activities	Engaged Math Activities
		Math Fact Time	Math Fact Time	Math Fact Time	Math Fact Time
	Group 2	Math Fact Time	Math Fact Time	Math Fact Time	Math Fact Time
		Guided Group	Guided Group	Guided Group	Guided Group
		Skills Review	Skills Review	Skills Review	Skills Review
		Engaged Math Activities	Engaged Math Activities	Engaged Math Activities	Engaged Math Activities
	Group 3	Skills review	Skills review	Skills review	Skills review
		Engaged Math Activities	Engaged Math Activities	Engaged Math Activities	Engaged Math Activities
		Math Fact Time	Math Fact Time	Math Fact Time	Math Fact Time
		Guided Group	Guided Group	Guided Group	Guided Group
	Group 4	Engaged Math Activities	Engaged Math Activities	Engaged Math Activities	Engaged Math Activities
		Math Fact Time	Math Fact Time	Math Fact Time	Math Fact Time
		Guided Group	Guided Group	Guided Group	Guided Group
		Skills Review	Skills Review	Skills Review	Skills Review

Made in the USA
Columbia, SC
19 July 2018